OF HORSE
I CAN

*Lessons of Success Straight
from the Horse's Mouth*

CATHY REILLY

ISBN: 979-8-89079-299-0 (ebook)
ISBN: 979-8-89079-297-6 (paperback)
ISBN: 979-8-89079-298-3 (hardback)

Jetlaunch Publishing

Heartfelt gratitude to Joanne and the Burg family for inviting me to vacation with you and taking me on my very first ride. Because of you, this wild, beautiful journey began.

To Susan—one of my bestest friends—thank you for convincing me to saddle up and take my first official lesson. Little did you know you'd be sparking a lifelong passion... and a few spectacular bruises along the way. That one nudge changed everything.

To my trainers, Chris and Nancy—the patient, persistent, and occasionally perplexed saints who taught me that falling off is just part of the process. Your guidance turned my flailing into finesse and my fears into fortitude. You laid the groundwork for every confident stride I take, in and out of the saddle.

To my family—my constant, unwavering support crew. You've cheered me on, picked me up (sometimes literally), and reminded me to keep riding when the trail got steep. Your love and encouragement have been what's kept the horse between me and the ground.

And finally... to every dirt-covered, tear-stained, joy-filled moment in this journey—I am grateful. You made me who I am. I wouldn't trade a single fall or flying leap for anything.

This ride's been wild. And it's just getting started.

Table of Contents

CHAPTER 1

Introduction

Lessons from the Saddle of Life

*H*ow *horses teach us more about ourselves than we ever expected.*

Imagine it: a warm summer's day in Hilton Head, South Carolina. Fresh off my first year at John Carroll University, I found myself whisked away for a week of fun with my friend Joanne and her family. Little did I know, that week would set the stage for a journey filled with unexpected twists and turns for years to come—a journey where my faithful companion, BeauJo, would take center stage.

Thunder, the horse assigned to me for that memorable trail ride, was a revelation. His calm demeanor and steady stride immediately put me at ease, igniting a spark of joy that stayed with me long after the ride ended. And as fate would have it, a fellow rider remarked on my "natural seat," planting the seed of a dream that would gradually take root.

Fast forward nearly a decade, and there I was, sharing hopes and dreams with my best friend Susan over drinks. Here we are, two Midwestern girls navigating the hustle and bustle of

Denver's legal scene, finding solace in each other's company. It was Susan who reignited my passion for riding, sparking a journey that would change my life in ways I never imagined.

What began as weekly lessons soon became a sanctuary—a place where the outside world faded away, leaving only the rhythmic sound of hoofbeats and the bond between horse and rider. But as my skills reached a plateau, I knew it was time for the next chapter—a chapter that would see me embark on the adventure of horse ownership.

Enter BeauJo, a spirited young gelding with a heart of gold and a world of potential. With the guidance of dedicated trainers and the support of newfound friends, we embarked on a journey that spanned over two decades—a journey filled with laughter, tears, and countless memories.

So, find your favorite spot, pour yourself a drink, and join me as I reminisce about the highs and lows of life with horses and my handsome "boyfriend" BeauJo. It's sure to be a ride you won't soon forget. Giddy up, and let's hit the trail together!

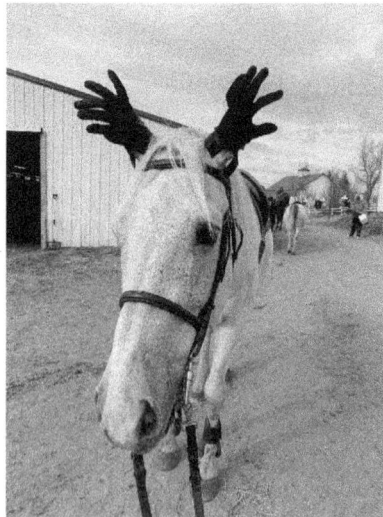

Giddy Up!

CHAPTER 2

Face Your Fear and Do It Scared

Fear isn't the end—it's the beginning of bold action.

I did it. I bought a horse.

Not just any horse—I added a tall, young, four-legged rocket launcher to my life. BeauJo was three years old, practically a toddler in horse years. Athletic, beautiful, full of potential… and still learning the ropes. So was I. And if I'm honest? I was scared out of my mind.

As a first-time horse owner, I had all the questions and none of the answers. What do I feed him? How do I train him? Is he safe to ride? What if he gets sick—wait, do horses even get sick? It was like bringing home a 1,200-pound toddler who could break your toe just by stepping a little too close.

So, I did what my litigation background taught me: I sought out the experts. I found a husband-and-wife training team who focused on developing both the horse and the rider.

Perfect. I'd learn the ropes while BeauJo grew into the partner I hoped he'd be.

And let me tell you—I was ready to do the work. My number one goal? Keep the horse between me and the ground.

In those early days, we trained five days a week. BeauJo and I worked together three of those, and he had two additional sessions focused on what they called "ground manners." Being orphaned as a foal, BeauJo hadn't had a mama horse to teach him how not to be a bull in a china shop. That meant we had to teach him: no nibbling, no crowding, no backing that booty into people. Basic boundaries. Essential lessons.

I loved every minute. But let's be real—I was chomping at the bit to ride. My trainers, though, were more focused on safety than speed. Smart. Annoying. Necessary.

So we lunged. A lot.

Lunging, if you're not familiar, is when the horse moves in a large circle around you on a long rope. You guide him with your voice, posture, and a lunge whip. It builds communication, burns energy, and teaches respect. "Master lunging," they said, "and riding will come easier."

BeauJo clearly didn't get the memo.

With my trainer, he was a rock star. With me? He acted like he couldn't hear a thing. For months, he'd stop, refuse to move, or pull little dominance games just to test my nerve. I was frustrated, embarrassed, and starting to wonder if I was the problem.

"Chris," I finally asked, "What am I doing wrong?"

He looked at me and said, "Nothing."

Then added, "But it's time you had a 'come to Jesus' moment with your horse."

Interesting, I thought.

Horses know what kind of energy you bring. They feel your hesitation, your nerves, your fear. BeauJo didn't need a buddy—he needed a boss. He needed to believe that the only

4

reason he was still upright was because I was having a good day. He needed to believe I was his Jesus.

What's on the other side of fear?

When you start something new as an adult—especially something physically demanding—your brain won't shut up. Adult brains are full of "what ifs," self-doubt, and worst-case scenarios. Kids don't think like that. Think skiing, skateboarding, biking. Kids are focused on the fun of it, not the fear.

Fear was holding me back.

So I asked myself: what do I show up for without fear? The answer was easy—my family.

What if I showed up for BeauJo the way I show up for my family? Fiercely. Fearlessly. Fully.

I realized I needed to change. I had to own the space, the mindset, the posture of being the boss. I had to let go of my fear.

The next few visits were different. I stopped letting BeauJo crowd me. I demanded stillness when I picked his feet. My energy shifted, and so did his.

One evening during lunging, he pulled the same tricks. But this time, it was in an arena full of other riders, and his antics started to cross the line into dangerous. My momma bear came out. I didn't flinch—I stepped forward with calm confidence and claimed my space.

It was our full-blown "come to Jesus" moment. His eyes widened. His posture softened. And right then, he knew. I was serious. I was his boss. I was his momma. I was his Jesus.

From that point forward, everything changed.

He started listening—not because I forced it, but because I earned it. We built trust. And I realized: facing my fear didn't give me control over him—it gave me control over how I showed up.

BeauJo, this powerful, breathtaking animal, wasn't my threat. He was my sanctuary. My freedom. But only once I dropped the fear.

Fear keeps us small.

It tells us we're not ready, that we're not enough. But fear is just a feeling—not a fact. And staying in fear? That's a choice. One that costs us more than we realize.

The first time I was asked to speak, fear showed up again.

I had overcome incredible adversity and was invited to share my story. My brain locked up. My throat dried out. I'm an introvert—I thrive behind the scenes. I'd built a career making lawyers shine in courtrooms… from the background.

Now I was being asked to take center stage and tell the story of how I nearly lost my life—and found my voice.

Fear owned me—until it didn't.

I said yes anyway. My face flushed, my ears burned, my heart pounded. But somewhere deep inside, I heard a whisper: *This means something big is about to happen.*

And I believed it.

I was on the edge—and I leaned in.

Because here's the truth:

Fear isn't a stop sign. It's a signal that you're growing.

You don't build confidence by waiting until you're ready. You build it by moving through the fear, step by shaky step.

You don't grow by sitting in the stands. You grow by taking the reins and showing up.

So here's your challenge:

Take a deep breath.

Find your 20 seconds of insane courage.

Say yes.

And go.

You don't need all the answers. You don't need perfection. You just need enough belief to take the first step.

Because everything you want? It's waiting for you—on the other side of fear.

Our first ride at our new barn - the journey begins

CHAPTER 3

Courage Leads the Way to Confidence

It's not just about bravery in the saddle—it's about trusting yourself enough to ride through the unknown.

E ver felt completely lost—no clue what you're doing—and desperately wishing someone would just hand you a map? Yep. Been there.

Horseback riding was my total unknown zone. And every ride felt like an open invitation to second-guess myself.

And that's exactly where courage comes in.

Courage doesn't wait for you to have all the answers. It's not about knowing the whole path—it's about taking the next step anyway. It's choosing to believe you'll figure it out, even when everything feels messy, hard, and completely out of your comfort zone.

When I first started riding, even learning the basics took courage. And jumping? Let's just say... it required multiple

20-second bravery windows. In fact, my first jumping lesson could've landed me on a blooper reel titled, "What NOT to Do on a Horse." Let me take you there.

We were in the arena—me, my trainer, and three other brave beginners. We'd spent the lesson working on our posting trot (you rise and sit with the rhythm of the horse's gait), and then the trainer introduced us to the three-point position. If you've ever seen jockeys ride—knees bent, seat off the saddle, leaning forward—that's the one. I loved it. The rhythm, the floating—it was like dancing on horseback.

Then came the big announcement: we'd be doing our first jump.

Cue the excitement... and panic.

I was first up. (Of course.)

I trotted confidently, locked into my rhythm, turned toward the jump, and felt my school horse start to lift. I was just sitting there thinking, *We're doing it!* like I was cruising through a drive-thru.

The horse jumped. I... kept going. Straight up.

Feet flew. Reins dropped. I went airborne like a cork from a champagne bottle. The horse landed like a pro. I landed like... well, a yoga mat burrito. Knees tucked, rolled, dirt in my teeth. I popped up, brushed off the dust, and blurted out, "What just happened?!"

My best friend was laughing so hard she couldn't breathe. And honestly? I earned every bit of it.

Turns out, my trainer had *assumed* I knew to switch from the posting trot into the three-point position before the jump. Assumptions + literal learners = liftoff.

That lesson taught me something powerful: courage means you'll mess up, fall down, and get back up anyway. It's never about perfect. It's about brave.

A few years later, after BeauJo joined my family, I had one of those full-circle moments.

My parents flew in from Ohio to visit us in Colorado. Now, we didn't grow up with horses. We were more about baseball, casseroles, and cousin chaos. So when I introduced them to BeauJo—this tall, majestic, muscular creature—they were floored.

During a family dinner back in Ohio later that year, someone asked my dad if he rode BeauJo.

"Heck no," he said. "That horse is a beast! But you should've seen Cathy. She handles that horse like he's a big ol' puppy—no hesitation, total control. She just bosses him around. And when he doesn't listen? She makes him! I wouldn't want to mess with her."

I was stunned.

My father really saw me.

And that moment stuck with me. Because for the first time, someone reflected back a version of me I hadn't fully seen yet: confident, calm, in control.

But here's the truth: that confidence didn't show up overnight. It was built—slowly, awkwardly, courageously.

Confidence comes after courage.

Courage is the spark.

Confidence is the fire.

You don't become confident by waiting until you feel ready. You become confident by doing the scary thing, falling on your butt, and choosing to brush yourself off and get back in the saddle. (Literally, in my case.)

Courage isn't the absence of fear. It's deciding to move forward while fear is still whispering in your ear. And every time you do, you chip away at that fear. You build muscle memory—not just in your body, but in your mind and heart too.

You start to trust yourself. You start to believe that maybe... just maybe...

You're stronger than you think.

And you are.

So, if you're standing at the edge of something right now—something big, bold, and maybe a little terrifying—hear me when I say:

> You don't need confidence to start.
> You need courage.
> Confidence will catch up.

> Take the jump.
> Fall down.
> Get up, laugh, and try again.

> And do it like you were born for it.
> Because you were.

As John Wayne famously said, *"Courage is being scared to death and saddling up anyway."*
So go ahead, saddle up, friend.
BeauJo says the ride of your life is waiting.

Helmuts required

CHAPTER 4

Size Doesn't Matter: Small Girl, Big Horse, Bigger Dreams

*It's not about how big you are –
it's about how big you dream.*

My entire life, I've been seated in the front row—not because I wanted to be first or the center of attention, but because I was short, petite, and, well... small. If you glance at any of my class pictures, there I am, right up front, legs crossed, hands clasped, smiling like I belonged there.

But the truth? I never felt like I was front-row material.

There's something about being small that makes you feel like you constantly have to prove yourself. Whether it was climbing shelves to reach the cereal box, being underestimated because of my size, or trying to speak louder in a room full of taller, more commanding voices (like my brothers), I often felt like I had to work twice as hard to measure up—literally and figuratively. I was used to being overlooked, used to people assuming I couldn't carry the weight (literal or metaphorical), and used to blending into the background... even if I was placed front and center.

And here's the kicker: when people underestimate you long enough, you start underestimating yourself, too.

It happens slowly, almost without you realizing it. At first, it's just an offhand comment—*You're too small to play. You don't seem capable. You're so quiet; are you sure you want to do it?* It doesn't feel like a big deal in the moment, but repetition is powerful. When people slap labels on you, when they define your limits for you, those limits start to feel real—even when they aren't. You absorb the words. You start shrinking into the space they say you belong in.

And you keep shrinking—until something (or someone) wakes you up and shakes you out of it.

> "The world will try to name you, box you in, and make you small. It's your job to refuse." — Unknown

For me, that wake-up call came in the form of a 1,200-pound horse. ·

Taking Up Space—And Owning It

BeauJo—my towering, majestic horse, and ironically, the greatest teacher I've ever had. Standing beside him, I looked like a child next to a giant. He was big. I was small. And everything about him reminded me of how far I felt from being confident, strong, and capable. At first, I doubted I could even control him.

How could someone my size command something so massive, so powerful?

But here's the thing: BeauJo didn't see my size. He saw my presence. He responded to my energy, my belief in myself—or lack thereof. And in that, he forced me to face a truth I'd spent years ignoring: I'd been playing small not because I was small, but because I had been convinced I should be.

Early on, I had no idea what I was doing. That's why I worked with a trainer—someone far more knowledgeable when it came to all things horse. The first thing we worked on? Ground manners. That means the way a horse behaves in the stall, when tied up, and when being led. The basics. The core foundation of respect between horse and rider.

And within the first month? BeauJo stepped on me and crushed my foot, ripping off my toenail.

Yep. Ouch.

That moment? Painful—and enlightening. It was my introduction to the importance of presence, space, and boundaries.

My trainer didn't sugarcoat it: "He's not paying attention to where his feet are because you're not paying attention to where yours are. You have to own your space." I had to learn how to say no—not with words, but with presence. I had to command space in a way BeauJo would understand.

If you've ever had kids or pets, you know that primal "mom" *NO* sound—the one that comes out when your toddler is about to stick something into a socket or the dog's about to swallow something they shouldn't. It's not polite—it's instinctual.

That was the sound I had to find.

Funny enough, once I nailed it, I started using it on my daughter... and my husband. (Don't tell them!)

It Was Never About My Size

Day by day, I realized something: BeauJo didn't need me to be big. He needed me to believe. He needed me to trust myself and show up with clarity and confidence. Because the moment I started owning my space—he responded in kind.

It wasn't about being stronger than him—because let's face it, he could take me—it was about trusting my own strength.

Horses are mirrors. They reflect what you bring. If you're unsure, they'll hesitate. If you're grounded, calm, clear? They'll follow.

And it's not just horses.

In life, just like in the barn, the same principle applies: It's not about being the biggest or the loudest—it's about showing up fully. Owning your voice. Holding your space. And daring to dream bigger than anyone expects you to.

That's why the phrase "front-row material" makes me laugh now. I used to be placed there because of my size. But now? I take the front row because I've earned it.

Starting with the End in Mind

My #1 goal was always to give BeauJo the best life. But along the way, he gave me one of the greatest gifts—the realization that showing up isn't about physical size. It's about presence.

BeauJo taught me that I didn't have to accept where life seated me—I could choose where I stood. And once I started dreaming bigger, I started living in alignment with those dreams. The goals I once tiptoed around became non-negotiable. I stopped shrinking. I stopped apologizing. I stood taller, spoke louder, and made choices with purpose.

As a mom, it meant modeling what strength and softness look like together. As a wife, it meant being an equal partner with an equal voice. And in business? It meant leading with both skill and soul—and never questioning whether I belonged at the table.

Owning the front row wasn't about ego—it was about setting the example. For others who've been told they're "too small," "too quiet," or "too much." It was about becoming the truest, fullest version of myself.

And here's the best part: once you start showing up for yourself like that? The world responds.

The opportunities I once thought were for someone else? They started showing up for me.

What About You?

Are you ready to stop shrinking? Are you ready to stop letting others define your space?

You don't need to be tall. Or loud. Or physically strong.

You just need to believe in your voice, your presence, and your power.

Because it's not about how big you are. It's about how boldly you dream.

How fiercely you live. And how bravely you show up.

So go ahead.

Stand up. Speak up. Saddle up.

Because you're not small.

You're mighty.

And the front row?

It's been waiting for you all along.

Big horse, small girl, so much love

CHAPTER 5

Always Check the Basics

The fundamentals aren't optional—they're essential.

When you start something—whether it's riding a horse, kicking off a new project, or walking into a meeting— it's tempting to rush in headfirst. We want to dive into the deep end, tackle the to-do list, or prove we're ready without thinking twice. But here's the deal: if you skip the basics, you're setting yourself up for unnecessary detours, wasted energy, and, let's be honest, maybe even a faceplant.

Trust me, I've learned this the hard way.

Check the Gas and Brakes

The first thing my trainer drilled into me was this: before you do anything else, check the basics. You have to be able to start and stop—no exceptions. Without that, you're toast.

So now, every single time I get on BeauJo, the very first thing I do is test those fundamentals. Can we start? Can we stop? These aren't just small details; they're everything. If

BeauJo isn't willing to move forward or halt when I ask, we've got a problem.

And here's the thing—I don't push through and hope for the best. I pause. I reassess. I fix it before moving on. Because if the basics aren't solid, nothing else will be. And in riding—as in life—that's the difference between a smooth ride and a disaster waiting to happen.

Disaster? Yep, that's one way to put it.

One late afternoon, eager to squeeze in a quick ride before an approaching storm, I rushed to the barn. The wind was picking up, dust was swirling, and the temperature was dropping. Determined to beat the weather, I tacked up BeauJo quickly and skipped our usual basic checks. I just wanted to get a workout in for him and a ride in for me.

From the start, BeauJo protested—ears pricked, muscles tense, clearly uneasy. Ignoring his signals, I pressed on.

Then, as if out of a movie, a tumbleweed blew past, spooking him and nearly unseating me. He jumped with all four legs in the air, and I popped off like a champagne cork. By some miracle, I landed back in the saddle—definitely not gracefully—and immediately knew I was going to feel that tomorrow.

His breathing grew loud and rapid. And in that moment, it hit me: I had skipped the basics. Those checks aren't just habits—they're communication. And I had ignored our connection.

The basics aren't just a checklist—they're the foundation of everything that follows. If we can't start or stop, how could I expect BeauJo to take on a new obstacle or pick up the pace?

Checking the basics isn't about rushing to the fun stuff. It's about setting us both up for success. When the foundation is solid, the ride becomes fun, free, and full of possibility.

The same principle applies to life. The basics are your foundation—the non-negotiables that prepare you for everything else. Whether it's a project, a conversation, or a personal goal, starting with the fundamentals ensures you're grounded.

Think of it like building a house. Would you skip the foundation and start with the walls? Of course not. A shaky foundation means cracks, instability, and trouble later. But when you start with strength underneath you, you can build as high as you dare to dream.

Take a Lap

Before hopping on BeauJo, I always take him for a walk around the arena. This routine helps us both scope out any new additions to the environment—like a stool in the corner or a hose that wasn't there yesterday. While I know these things are harmless, to BeauJo, they're potential "horse eaters."

Horses are naturally cautious and often see unfamiliar objects as threats. It's my job to show him he's safe. That initial lap helps him settle in and helps me check in with his energy. By the time we mount, we're already in sync.

Before jumping into anything—a meeting, a project, even a party—it's smart to "walk the arena" first. Take a moment to observe who's there, sense the vibe, and get your bearings.

My daughter once referenced a high school movie where the main character advises a newcomer to take a lap before settling in at a party. Honestly? That's solid life advice.

Why the Basics Matter

Skipping the basics might feel like you're saving time—but really, you're setting yourself up for a stumble. The basics ground you. They give you the clarity, confidence, and presence to handle whatever comes next.

Whether it's a literal lap around the arena or a mental check-in, taking that moment makes a world of difference.

- **In your personal life**: Before having a tough conversation, ask yourself if you're in the right headspace. If not, pause. Take a breath.
- **In your professional life**: Before launching a new initiative, check your timeline, resources, and team. Is everything aligned?
- **In social settings**: Before diving in, scan the room. Feel the energy. Acclimate. Show up in a way that feels true to you.

Give Yourself Permission to Pause

It's perfectly okay to recognize when you're not ready to move forward. Whether it's realizing your "gas and brakes" aren't responding, sensing a storm rolling in, or simply needing a minute—pausing isn't weakness. It's wisdom.

After learning that lesson the hard way, I made it a priority to always check the basics with BeauJo. There were times I could feel something was off, and instead of pushing through, I dismounted. We'd spend time walking or grooming instead. And almost every time, I later discovered why—maybe he'd been injured in turnout, or had a sore in his mouth. The pause always proved right.

Sometimes, the kindest thing we can do—for ourselves or others—is honor what's needed in the moment, even if that means changing the plan.

So, the next time you're about to dive into something big—whether it's a business venture, a relationship conversation, or simply your day—remember:

- **Check your gas and brakes**. Are you ready to move and stop when needed?
- **Take a lap**. Get the lay of the land before you dive in.
- **Honor the basics**. They're not just for beginners. They're for champions.

"Success is the sum of small efforts, repeated day in and day out." — Robert Collier

By focusing on those small, consistent practices, we set ourselves up for steady progress, fewer surprises, and more wins.
Take your time. Check in. Get clear. Then saddle up.
Because when you honor the basics, the rest of the ride becomes magic.

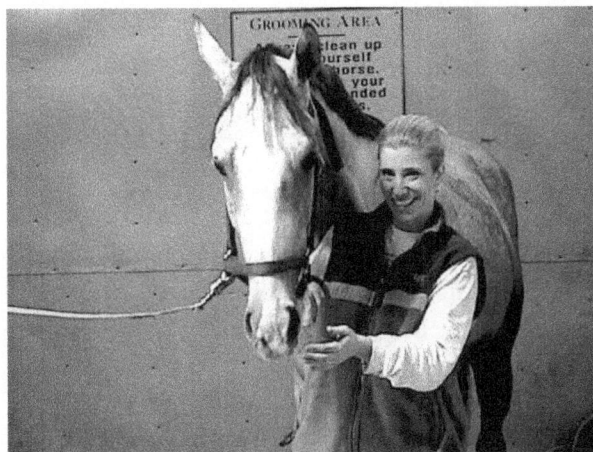

Giving BeauJo his first bath

CHAPTER 6

Strong Core, Strong Rider, Stronger You

Build your core—physically,
mentally, and emotionally.

When I first started riding, I assumed staying on a horse was all about gripping with my legs. I pictured those old Westerns, where cowboys dismount with that telltale bowlegged swagger. I figured squeezing with everything I had was the key to staying put.

Spoiler alert: that's not how it works.

Turns out, your legs are more about steering. Crazy, right? Picture a drunken sailor—that was me and my horse, zigzagging all over the place until I finally grasped the real dynamics. My trainers constantly chided, "Too much leg!" and repeated, "Ride from your core!" But what does that even mean?

Riding from my core didn't make sense—until it did.

Engaging Your Core

Let me paint you a picture. Imagine trying to grip a chair with your butt. Go ahead, give it a try—I know you're curious. Feels a bit odd, doesn't it? Well, that's pretty much how you hold on to a horse. It's not about clinging desperately with your legs (which, fun fact, just signals the horse to go faster). The real strength lies in your core—your seat, lower back, and abdomen. That's where your balance, stability, and control come from.

Engaging your core not only stabilizes your position but also allows for subtle communication with your horse, leading to a more harmonious ride.

Let me be real: my number one goal with riding has always been to keep the horse between me and the ground. That's it. If I could stay on and avoid a dirt nap, I considered it a win. And in those early days, it wasn't pretty. Every single muscle in my core ached after my first lesson. Muscles I didn't even know I had screamed at me for days. Balancing in the saddle, keeping weight in my heels, and finding that even seat—it was a lot to think about, and it felt nearly impossible at first.

Over time, though, something incredible happened. Those muscles that were weak and unused began to build. I wasn't thinking so much about gripping and balancing anymore—my body just knew. My seat became steadier, and I started riding with more ease. But here's the thing: even when you've built those muscles, you can't stop. Riding takes constant practice. If you get complacent, you lose that strength.

And when you think about it, it's the same in life.

Engaging Your Core in Life

Just as your physical core keeps you balanced and upright in the saddle, your core values keep you steady and grounded in your decisions. They're the foundation that guides you, shapes your choices, and helps you navigate life's challenges.

But just like riding, living in alignment with your core values isn't always easy.

There was a time in my life when I was running what looked like a successful business. From the outside, everything seemed great—the revenue was there, the clients were coming in, the wheels were turning. But inside? I felt stuck. Like I'd hit an invisible glass ceiling I couldn't break through. No matter how hard I worked, I couldn't seem to take things to the next level.

Then God stepped in.

The doors to that business closed, and almost simultaneously, I faced my first major health crisis. Both events forced me to pause, reflect, and reimagine what I was doing.

At first, I was devastated. I questioned everything—my purpose, my worth, whether I'd ever be able to rebuild. But looking back, I see now those closed doors and that health scare were gifts. That business wasn't aligned with my core values, and the health wake-up call reminded me: life is too short to keep pushing down the wrong path.

When I finally got clear on my values, everything shifted. I realized I had been holding myself back—trying to build something that didn't reflect who I truly was. I was out of balance, gripping too hard with the wrong muscles, forgetting the power of my core.

Now, every decision I make—whether in business, parenting, or my personal life—is grounded in those values. They're my anchor, my compass, and my fuel.

Your core values work the same way. They're the muscles that keep you steady when life throws curveballs. They help you stand tall, move forward with purpose, and stay balanced through the messy middle.

But like any muscle, they need intentional effort to grow and stay strong. You can't just name them once and call it good. You have to live them. Practice them. Strengthen them. Every day.

Just like riding a horse, staying connected to your core values takes time, patience, and repetition. But the payoff? It's everything. When you live in alignment with your values, you ride through life with more ease, confidence, and joy.

How to Identify Your Core Values

If you're not sure what your core values are, here's a simple, powerful exercise I guide my clients through:

1. **Create Two Lists**:

   o Joyful Activities: List everything that brings you joy—those activities that light you up, moments that fill your cup, and experiences that make you genuinely happy.

   o Draining Activities: On the other side, jot down things that make you anxious or unhappy—tasks you dread, situations you'd rather avoid, and experiences you'd be glad to leave behind.

2. **Identify Patterns**:

   o Examine both lists to spot common themes. The joyful list might reveal values like creativity, connection, or adventure, while the draining list could highlights tress, competition, or pressure.

3. **Compare with Core Values List**:

   ○ Match these patterns to a core values list, such as the one available on my website at www.freegift-fromcathy.com. This comparison can help you pinpoint the values that truly resonate with you.

4. **Select Your Top 3-5 Values**:

   ○ From your reflections, identify the top 3-5 values that stand out. These form the foundation of your core values – your nonnegotiables. Remember, they may evolve over time, but they represent your current guiding principles.

How to Identify Your Core Values

Building strength—in riding or life—isn't about perfection. It's about intention. Grace. Consistency. And the willingness to wobble a little as you grow.

The more you engage your core—physically and metaphorically—the more powerful, grounded, and capable you'll become.

"Learning patience can be a difficult experience, but once conquered, you will find life is easier." — Catherine Pulsifer

So sit tall. Breathe deep. Trust your seat.

Because a strong core builds a strong rider. And a strong rider becomes an stronger human.

Engaging my core and riding a ride

CHAPTER 7

The Tools of the Trade

In life and riding, the right tools set you up for success.

How much do you value your pooper?

Yep, I said it. Bear with me.

When I first started riding, I used a standard-issue saddle—the kind you'd find in any lesson barn. It wasn't fancy, just functional. But it felt more suited for someone taller. I often found myself tipping backward like the Leaning Tower of Pisa. As BeauJo and I logged more hours together, I realized "good enough" wasn't going to cut it. So, I invested in a saddle tailored specifically for both of us.

The transformation? Wow.

Not only did it improve my posture and comfort, but it benefited BeauJo, too—ensuring better weight distribution and less pressure on his back. This wasn't just a splurge; it was an investment in our partnership. The right tools didn't just boost our ride—they transformed it.

And speaking of transformation...

In those early days, BeauJo had one gear: fast. The boy had a *need for speed*. I did *not*. He loved pushing forward, always eager to see how fast we could go while I was still trying to find my balance. Riding him felt like a roller coaster without a lap bar. And when he jumped? He didn't just leap—he launched.

Something had to change.

With my trainer's guidance, we started researching bits. If you're not familiar, a bit is part of a horse's bridle and sits in that gummy space between their front and back teeth. It's a key communication tool—one that can either build trust or cause frustration, depending on the fit.

After some trial and error, we found the perfect one. It gave me just enough control to gently guide BeauJo without throwing off my balance or hurting his mouth. That small piece of equipment became a total game-changer for us. We moved in sync. The frustration faded. And riding became fun again.

Sometimes, the smallest adjustments make the biggest impact.

Equipment in Life: Your People

In riding and in life, the most important "equipment" isn't made of leather or metal. It's your people.

Just like the wrong saddle can make a ride painful, the wrong people can make your life harder. As Jim Rohn famously said, *"You are the average of the five people you spend the most time with."*

Let's break that down:

Your circle *matters*.

Positive, growth-minded people raise your energy. They inspire and support you. On the flip side? One toxic, draining person can derail your momentum.

So how do you know if your people are the right ones?

Ask yourself:

- Do they light you up or wear you down?
- Do they celebrate your wins and sit with you during the hard stuff?
- Do they challenge you in the best way?

Your body will tell you. Trust the vibe.

When you're with the right people, you feel energized, grounded, and like your most authentic self.

Not everyone belongs in the front row of your life.

Some folks belong in the balcony—or maybe even outside the building. And that's okay. This isn't about cutting people off with scissors and sass (unless you need to). It's about adjusting how much access they have to your energy.

Protect your peace.

Surround yourself with the right people—the ones who lift, align, and support your journey.

The Power of Alignment

Just like finding the right saddle took time, curating your inner circle takes intention. But once everything clicks into place?

You ride smoother.

You live stronger.

You lead better.

So, invest in your tools—both the gear and the people.

Take stock of what supports you and what doesn't.

Upgrade as needed.

Because whether you're riding a horse or steering your life, one truth holds:

The right tools—and the right people—make all the difference.

My daughter Jackie learning to ride – note the helmet and gloves

CHAPTER 8

Bridging the Gap

Mastering communication with horses and humans.

Imagine this—it's early morning, the sun just beginning to peek over the horizon, and the air feels crisp and alive. The only sound is the soft whinny of BeauJo as he spots me approaching the barn. My heart skips a beat, and a smile spreads across my entire body. This is our time—just me and my horse. From the moment I step into the stables to the moment I leave, we're in constant conversation. And he's speaking right back to me.

Horses don't use words, but trust me—they have *a lot* to say. BeauJo picks up on everything: my energy, my attitude, and even my "stinkin' thinkin'." Whatever's going on in my head, he feels it like I've posted it on a billboard just for him. And just as he picks up on me, I pick up on him—his body language, his breath, the position of his ears. Every movement, every shift is a message.

BeauJo is my therapy, my sanctuary, my peace. He pulls me out of the chaos in my head and calls me back to presence.

Because when you're with a horse, there's no multitasking. No mental to-do list. No drama from yesterday or worry about tomorrow. There's only *now*.

When You're Off, They Know It

I remember one day in particular when I showed up at the barn after a rough day at work. My mind was swirling with stress and "what-ifs." I went through the motions—checked the basics, tacked up, started our warmup—but I wasn't really *there*. And BeauJo knew it.

He was off—tense, distracted, resistant—but I was too wrapped up in my own head to notice. As we rode, the disconnect grew. He pulled on the reins, picked up speed, and wasn't responding to my cues. I got frustrated. "Why is he being such a pill?" I thought. I blamed him, but deep down, I knew the truth.

The battle wasn't with BeauJo—it was with *me*. I wasn't present. I wasn't clear. And he was simply responding to the chaos I brought into the arena.

Finally, I stopped. Took a deep breath. And realized what was happening. I apologized—not with words, but with a softer presence. A slower breath. A calming energy. He exhaled right along with me.

We started over.

And those next 20 minutes? Pure magic. We moved in sync, not because I demanded it, but because I showed up differently. Fully. Calmly. With heart.

I wish I could say I learned my lesson that day and it never happened again. But let's be real—I'm human. And being present is an art form. Every ride, every conversation, every day—it takes work.

BeauJo taught me this: when you're off, the world around you feels it. Whether it's a horse, a coworker, a partner, or your kid, the energy you bring matters. Your presence matters. When you show up fully, that's when the connection clicks—and the real magic begins.

Communication Is More Than Words

Whether you're working with a horse or talking with a friend, communication is so much more than just *what* you say. Studies show that only 7% of communication is verbal. The rest? It's tone, posture, facial expressions, and energy.

Horses don't care about your words—they care about your vibe. Are you calm or agitated? Focused or distracted? Grounded or flighty? They read it all. So do people.

You can say all the right things, but if your energy doesn't match—if your tone or body language is off—it won't land. People and horses respond more to *how* you make them feel than what you say.

Build Your Communication Muscles

Let me take you on a little detour.

Prince Charming and I were trying to expand our family. After years of infertility, tests, and specialists, we finally had our daughter through IVF. A couple of years later, we tried again—same route. Same hopes. Same heartbreak.

One February, Prince Charming and our daughter went skiing, and I stayed home. That morning, I bent down and *POP*—a sound, a feeling, and then a slow-growing pain that took over my entire body. By nightfall, I was in the ER, doubled over, barely conscious.

The doctors buzzed around me like bees, asking questions, poking, prodding. I was too dazed to respond. My husband stood next to me, grounded and calm, holding space when I couldn't.

Then the doctor came in with urgency. "Could you be pregnant?"

"No," I said. "That's not possible."

But it was. And it wasn't. I was pregnant—with an ectopic pregnancy. And the moment I heard the word "pregnant," something inside me lit up. For a brief, blissful moment, I thought *maybe*... maybe I'd get to carry another baby.

When I asked, "Will the medication hurt the baby?" the room went completely silent.

Everyone's face dropped.

And that silence? It spoke volumes.

That's when I knew. Not a viable pregnancy. I said it aloud so they didn't have to. Everyone exhaled, and the doctor moved forward.

That moment will stay with me forever—not just for the heartbreak, but for the clarity it brought. In life, the most powerful communication often isn't verbal. It's in the silence. The stillness. The presence.

Practice Brings Progress

Strong communication takes practice, presence, and patience. It's not about being perfect—it's about showing up with intention. Whether you're in the saddle, at the dinner table, or leading a meeting, here are a few ways to grow your communication muscle:

1. **Be Present**: Whether you're talking to a person or working with a horse, focus fully on the interaction.

Put your phone away, quiet your inner dialogue, and give your full attention to the moment.

2. **Pay Attention to Nonverbals**: Notice your body language, tone of voice, and facial expressions. Are they aligned with the message you're trying to send?

3. **Listen Actively**: Communication isn't just about talking—it's about listening. With horses, this means observing their movements, energy, and responses. With people, it means truly hearing what they're saying without planning your next response.

4. **Recheck and Adjust**: If something feels off, pause and reassess. Just like I had to pause with BeauJo and start over, sometimes you need to hit the reset button in conversations to realign.

Communication Is Connection

At its core, communication is connection. It's trust. It's presence. It's the unspoken truth exchanged in a glance, a breath, a shared rhythm.

So whether you're in the arena with a horse or at home with your family, remember this:

It's not just *what* you say.
It's *how* you show up.

Speak with intention.
Listen with empathy.
And show up with heart.

Because when your presence aligns with your message? That's when the magic happens.

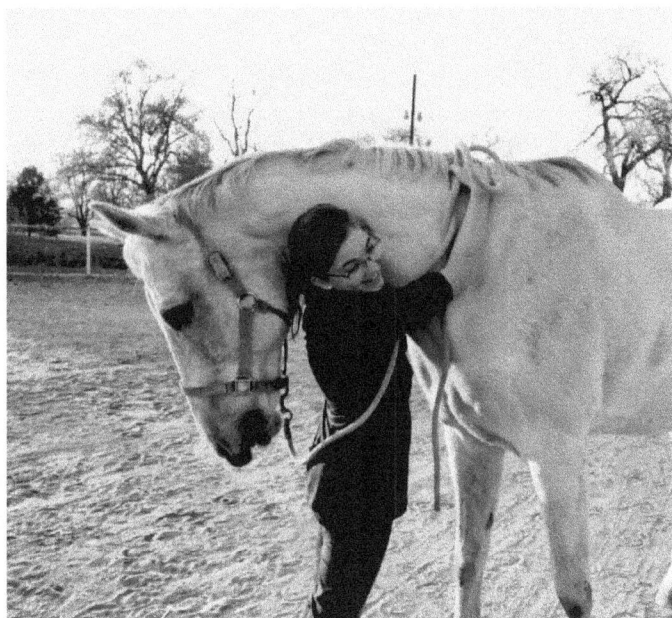

BeauJo hugs are the best!

CHAPTER 9

Where Focus Goes, Energy Flows

Harness the power of intention in riding and for your life.

Anne Lamott said it best: "Almost everything will work again if you unplug it for a few minutes, including you." That was my Sundays. My sacred time to reboot, recharge, and remember who I was—beyond the emails, deadlines, and endless to-do lists.

In those early years of riding, I was married, working long hours in litigation (which, by the way, never sleeps and never slows down), and constantly tethered to my phone. Emails didn't stop on weekends, and neither did the pressure to be available. But Sundays? Sundays were mine.

That's when I had my riding lessons. For nearly four years, like clockwork, every Sunday I fed my passion for horses and gave myself permission to get dirty and just *be*. With a big ol' smile on my face, I'd tack up whatever school horse I was assigned and head into the arena.

I always arrived early to snag at least ten peaceful minutes to walk the horse around the arena—my own little warm-up before the real work began. Then came the lesson, usually alongside a small group of women just like me—learning to ride, learning to breathe again, and maybe even learning to live a little louder.

Our trainer would call out commands like a conductor directing a symphony: turn this circle, cross the diagonal, approach the poles, change direction, change gait. She'd tell us what to do—walk, trot, canter—and where to do it. Just when we'd get comfortable, she'd mix it up to keep both us and the horses sharp. Honestly, I loved it. I didn't have to make decisions—my brain was fully booked focusing on my seat, my legs, and my hands.

But then came the one command that used to drive me absolutely bananas:

Eyes forward!

I'd be deep in a turn, laser-focused—or so I thought—when she'd yell, "Eyes forward!" And in my head, dripping with sarcasm, I'd think, *Where else would I be looking, lady? I'm literally on the front of this horse.* Like clockwork, my body would tense with frustration.

Then she'd follow it with the ever-helpful: *Breathe.*

Let's be honest—for most of us, being told to "breathe" right after getting corrected feels like being told to "calm down" in an argument. Spoiler alert: it doesn't help.

Until it does.

Until one day, it finally clicked.

That day, after the same cue for what felt like the hundredth time, I paused mid-lesson and turned to my trainer.

"What exactly do you mean by *eyes forward*?" I asked. "Because I think I'm doing it right—and clearly, I'm not."

That question changed everything.

She explained that "eyes forward" wasn't just about looking ahead—it was about looking where I *wanted* to go. The next jump. The next marker. The next goal. What I had been doing was looking just a few feet in front of BeauJo—right between his ears. And that meant my focus, and my ride, were getting stuck in the short term.

To make her point, she walked out into the arena and stood exactly where I should be looking.

As I trotted toward her, something shifted. I could feel the change in my posture, in the horse's movement, in how the ride flowed. All from simply shifting my focus.

Success. That revelation was a game-changer.

As someone who tends to take things literally, that simple adjustment—looking ten feet ahead instead of three—transformed the ride. My body adjusted in anticipation. My balance improved. BeauJo relaxed. We found rhythm. We found connection. And all because I finally started focusing on where I wanted to go.

Life Flows Where Focus Goes

A slight shift in focus can transform your ride. And just like in the arena, a slight shift in perspective can profoundly impact your life.

Let me paint you a picture:

An elderly professor, reminiscent of Albert Einstein with unruly white hair and thick glasses, walked into a bustling classroom of teens. He quietly approached the chalkboard and began writing:

7 + 3 = 10
12 + 5 = 17
9 + 6 = 15
15 + 4 = 19
8 + 2 = 10

The classroom remained silent, the students watching intently but offering no reaction. Then, on the final problem, the professor wrote:

5 + 9 = 13

A ripple of giggles and whispers spread through the room. The students couldn't contain their amusement at the apparent mistake. The professor turned to face them, his eyes twinkling with wisdom. He calmly addressed the class:

"I've presented several correct equations, yet none of you reacted. It was only when I made a mistake that you found your voice. This illustrates an important lesson: our minds often fixate on what's wrong, overlooking the multitude of things that go right."

The room fell silent as the students absorbed the significance of his words.

Life Flows Where Focus Goes

What's the best thing that happened to you today? This month? This year?

And be honest—how often are you actually thinking about that?

I get it. You're busy. You're juggling a hundred things, wearing all the hats, carrying the weight of the world on your shoulders—and still showing up with a smile. I see you.

But how often do you catch yourself saying, "I don't have time," or "I wish I had more hours in the day"? Or maybe, "I'll do it when things slow down," as if that magical moment is just around the corner?

Here's the truth bomb: That kind of thinking is a Catch-22. The way our brains work, when we tell ourselves we don't have time, we're too busy, or we just can't do it right now, our brain goes, "Got it!"—and finds ways to prove us right. So what happens? We never "find" the time, because we're not looking for it—we're focused on not having it.

Your brain is like a supercomputer, quietly tracking every word, thought, and belief you feed it. And here's the kicker: it's designed to prove you right. So when you say, "I'm too busy," it says, "You got it!" and keeps you in that cycle.

But flip the script? Shift the focus? That's when the magic happens.

Because life flows where focus goes. Want more time, energy, joy, peace, success—whatever it is? Start focusing on that. Speak it. Think it. Believe it. Your brain will catch on and start looking for ways to deliver it.

Flip the Script

In riding, I discovered that shifting my focus—looking ahead to where I wanted to go—transformed my experience in the saddle. By directing my gaze toward the next jump or marker, my body naturally adjusted, aligning with BeauJo's movements and creating a smoother, more harmonious ride.

Life works the same way.

Instead of fixating on the chaos or the fear, choose a better focus. Want more time? Focus on what you *can* do, not what you can't. Want more peace? Focus on what's already calm. Want more success? Start with what's already working.

It's called rescripting—replacing those old, tired, fear-based beliefs with something stronger. Something *true*.

And that's how you start to train your brain to look for what's right, not just what's wrong.

Just like my ride with my horse smoothed out the moment I shifted my gaze, your life will flow more easily when your energy matches your intention.

So Let Me Ask You...

Where are you looking right now?

Are you staring between your horse's ears—focused on what's right in front of you? Or are you lifting your eyes, setting your sights, and aligning yourself with where you *really* want to go?

Your focus is your compass.

Your energy is your fuel.

Your intention is your map.

Point them in the right direction—and then ride like you mean it.

Because where focus goes, energy flows.

And my friend?

The view ahead is worth it.

Taking a moment to enjoy the ride.

CHAPTER 10

Do The Dang Thing

It's not just what you know—it's what you do with it.

Ever found yourself thinking, *What am I doing?*

In the spring of 2002, a mutual friend introduced me to a tall, young gray gelding who immediately captured my attention. He was inquisitive, athletic, and had a quiet intensity that felt different from any horse I'd met before. When I climbed into the saddle, something shifted. Despite his minimal training, his canter was astonishingly smooth—like gliding over calm waters.

After our ride, we stood together in the stall, our foreheads gently touching, breaths harmonizing. In that quiet moment, our eyes met, and an unspoken bond formed. I knew I wanted him, and cautiously entered the prepurchase process—hoping the vet would give us the green light.

On June 28, 2002, Encore Beaujolais—affectionately known as BeauJo—came home. I became his forever momma.

My dream had come true.

And then... the flood of questions began:

How much should he eat? What kind of supplements does he need? Is he okay with turnout? Does he like other horses?

The list went on. And the stress? Oh, it matched any major life milestone—buying a house, getting married, starting a family.

Because the truth? I didn't know much beyond what I'd read in books or seen from afar. What in the world had I gotten myself into?

But that's the moment I learned something life-changing:

Knowledge is power—only when you put it into action.

So I dove in. I read every horse care book I could find. I asked endless questions. I leaned on seasoned pros and worked closely with a training couple who specialized in young horses. But reading about horse care isn't the same as doing it. I had to show up. Muck the stalls. Fill the buckets. Pick the hooves. Learn the body language. Catch the signals. Build the bond. Again and again.

Every single day with BeauJo was a classroom. And every moment—sometimes graceful, often messy—turned information into insight.

Practice became progress.

Because this wasn't just a hobby or a phase. This was a life-changing journey. So I did something very "me": I started journaling. I wanted to remember it all—the wins, the wipeouts, the awkward in-betweens. On July 8, 2002, BeauJo and I had our first official riding lesson together.

That's when the real growth began.

My trainer brought the wisdom.

I brought the curiosity and the grit.

BeauJo brought the heart.

And together, we began building something beautiful—one ride at a time.

No One Starts as an Expert

Let me say it again for the people in the back: *I had no idea what I was doing.*

I didn't know horses teethe like toddlers. I didn't know his endless energy wasn't just excitement—it was a baby horse being a baby horse. I didn't know the basics of hoof care, how often they need trims, what vaccinations to track, or how often to check his feed and tack.

And I definitely didn't know how much pain one toe could cause when a 1,200-pound animal steps on it. (Spoiler alert: a *lot.* Lost the toenail. Gained a life lesson.)

I was learning. All of it. Slowly, imperfectly, one saddle-sore step at a time.

I learned how to ride around others. How to jump. How to move barns. How to welcome other riders who would lease him. How to grow old with him—with patience, with grace, with more love than I knew possible.

And every step of the way, I kept journaling:

- 7/2002 – Young horses need to investigate things. They don't know trash cans, dogs, chairs, mirrors, or floating leaves. Let him check it out—he's not being dramatic, he's being a horse.
- 8/2002 – Kids scare him, and he loves baths… so much that I end up just as soaked.
- 9/2002 – Horses need their feet trimmed every six weeks. Noted.
- 10/2002 – A freshly bathed horse will *absolutely* roll in the mud the second you turn your back.
- 11/2002 – Saw a woman riding her horse while talking on the phone. #Goals.

49

- 12/2002 – Vaccines and health checks happen twice a year. Check.
- 1/2003 – New year, new me, new us. Giddy up.

It wasn't always pretty. But it was always real.

Stop Waiting. Start Doing.

If I had waited until I had all the answers, I never would have brought BeauJo home. I never would've learned everything he came to teach me. I would have missed the single most transformative experience of my life.

So let me ask you:

What are you waiting for?

What decision are you putting off until you "know more," "feel ready," or "have it all figured out"?

Spoiler alert: that moment may never come.

You don't need more information. You need more action. You need to *do the thing*. Make the move. Ask the question. Take the leap. Trust that you'll figure it out on the way down.

Because here's the thing…

It's not what you know that changes your life—it's what you do with it.

Growth doesn't live in perfection.

It lives in motion.

In trying.

In getting back up after the not-so-graceful fall.

In building muscle—not just in your body, but in your courage.

Snapshot of a Beginning

That fall, I hired a professional photographer to capture our new beginning. Not because we were polished or perfect—but because I wanted to remember what it looks like to say *yes* to something before you're ready.

That photo still lives in my wallet today. A reminder of the moment I chose faith over fear. The moment I became a horse mom. The moment everything changed.

From Knowledge to Wisdom

Wisdom doesn't come from knowing.
It comes from *doing*.
It's built in the saddle.
In the journaling.
In the messy middle.
In the grit and grace of showing up—especially when you're unsure.

So stop waiting for the day you'll "know enough."

Start where you are.
With what you have.
And trust that the rest will meet you on the trail.

You won't always get it right.
But you will grow.
And isn't that the point?

So saddle up, friend.

The journey doesn't start when you know enough.
It starts when you say yes anyway.

The day I looked at BeauJo and he looked at me, and we said yes.

CHAPTER 11

Patience is Your Superpower

Big things take time—embrace the wait.

Let's be real—starting something new can be equal parts exhilarating and exasperating. If you're anything like me, you dive in headfirst, full of energy and expectation... and then get frustrated when you're not instantly great at it. Sound familiar?

Now, I live with someone who makes everything look effortless. My husband? Yeah, he's *that* guy. The one who picks up a new skill like he's done it a hundred times. I'll never forget when we took our four-year-old daughter ice skating on the frozen lake in Evergreen.

Picture it: a crisp Colorado day, sunshine bouncing off the ice, excitement in the air. I laced up, channeling my inner roller-skating child of the '80s, fully prepared to giggle as my husband—who claimed he'd *never* skated before—clumsily flailed around.

Except... he didn't. He glided. Gracefully. Effortlessly. Holding our daughter's hand like a Hallmark movie hero.

When I asked him how many times he'd been on the ice, he shrugged and said, "Never."

Never?!

That's when I realized—he's got natural athletic ability that could make the rest of us roll our eyes and question all our life choices.

Me? Not so much. I wasn't the first picked for any team. In fact, if we're being honest, I was thrilled just to be *picked*. Sports were never my thing. Coordination? Questionable.

But horses? Now, that was different.

The one thing that's always felt natural for me was sitting on a horse. Something about it just clicked. Being up there felt like home. Balanced. Peaceful. Right. But let's not get it twisted—sitting on a horse and actually *riding* one? Not the same thing.

I took riding lessons for four years before BeauJo came into my life, and even then, I was still a beginner. Green is what they call a newbie rider. I was definitely green, not just because I was new but also because I was so envious of everyone looking like experts. I thought I'd learn everything I needed in that first year of owning him. (Bless my ambitious little heart.) Boy was I mistaken. We'd have a great lesson one day, and I'd feel on top of the world. Then the next? Total chaos. It felt like everything fell apart and I'd forgotten how to ride altogether.

Welcome to growth—it's not linear, it's a roller coaster with no seatbelt.

Let's Talk About Hands

You'd think hand placement would be easy, right? Nope.

In English-style riding, your hands are the heart of your communication with your horse. They need to be:

- **Elbows**: Soft bend, close to your sides—like you're holding a secret and don't want to spill it.
- **Hands**: Floating just above the saddle, about four inches apart, in front of the withers. Not too high, not too low.
- **Thumbs**: Pointing upward, like you're about to pass the tiniest salt shaker ever.
- **Grip**: Gentle but steady—no death grip allowed.

Now imagine trying to do all that *while* engaging your core, swinging your hips, staying balanced, watching your breathing... and trotting on a thousand-pound animal with opinions.

It's a lot. And none of it feels natural at first.

There were so many moments I wanted to scream, "How can this still be so hard?! Shouldn't this be easier by now?"

Riding Is Like Golf

The best comparison I can give? Golf.

Golf is maddening. Every round is different. Every swing is unique. Just when you think you've got it—*you don't*. It's all timing, rhythm, and balance. No two shots are ever the same.

Riding is the same way—only you're not just dealing with yourself. You've got a living, breathing creature under you who's

55

having a day of his own. You're building trust, communication, rhythm. And some days? That rhythm is off. And that's okay.

Time Off and a Hard Lesson

When I became pregnant, I had to take time off riding. That was tough. BeauJo was my therapy. My peace. So I still went to the barn just to be near him. I found a few wonderful women to lease him while I was out of the saddle, and they kept him fit and fulfilled.

But when I returned? Everything felt off. I was different. He was different. So I booked a lesson with a highly respected trainer at our barn.

Only two of us were in the lesson, so I was getting a lot of personal attention—lucky me!

Now, BeauJo is a tall boy, and I'm... not. I used short, stubby spurs—not to be harsh, but just as a subtle cue to extend my natural leg. I didn't love using a crop, and the trainer respected my choice, even though it wasn't her preferred tool.

But during this lesson, BeauJo wasn't listening. At all. He ignored my cues. Missed transitions. I was frustrated. He was frustrated.

The trainer paused us and asked, "When your daughter doesn't respond right away, what do you do? Do you poke her?"

"Of course not," I said.

"Then why aren't you giving BeauJo the same grace?"

Mic. Drop.

That moment cracked me wide open. She wasn't just talking about horses—she was talking about life. About communication. About empathy.

Sometimes, it's not about how your horse responds—it's about how you *ask*.

I took off my spurs. We started over. This time, I slowed my ask:

- Ask once—no response.
- Ask again—a little firmer. He considered it.
- Ask a third time—calmly, clearly. He trotted.

We tried again. And again. By the third round, he responded immediately. No hesitation. We were back in sync.

It wasn't about domination. It was about trust. It took space, grace, and patience.

Grace Is a Game-Changer

That lesson stuck. Whenever we got out of sync after that, I remembered: pause, breathe, offer grace. To him—and to me.

They say it takes 21 days to build a habit. But let's be real: the ones that matter? The ones that require your *whole self*—your heart, your energy, your intention—those take longer.

They take patience.

Developing Patience (and a Better Seat)

One of the first tools I learned in riding was breathing. And years later, I finally understood its power—not just in the saddle, but in life.

Breath anchors you. It brings you back to now. Studies show deep breathing can reduce anxiety, center your mind, and help your body reset.

So whether you're learning to ride, building a business, raising a child, or trying to keep it together... breathe.

Let your inhale create space.

Let your exhale bring clarity.
You don't need to rush. You don't need to be perfect.
You just need to keep showing up.

Patience Isn't Passive—It's Powerful

And when you give yourself grace… when you trust the process… when you stick with it even when it's messy?
That's when the magic happens.
You're doing better than you think.
You're allowed to be a work in progress.
And you've got a superpower in your back pocket.
It's called *patience*.
Use it well.

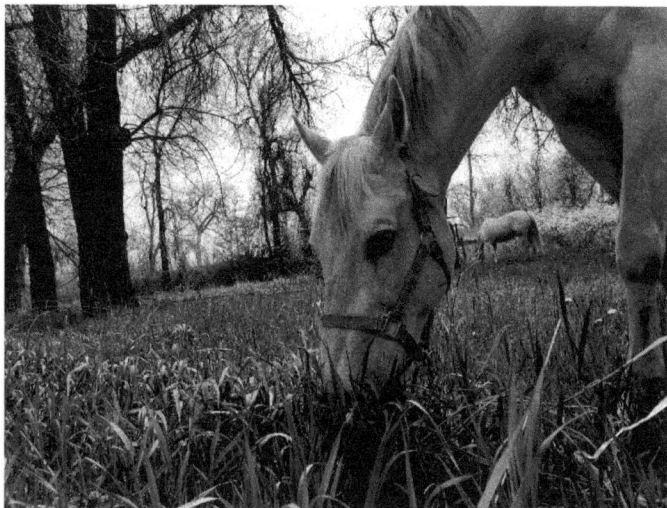

There's a time to ride, a time to breathe, and a time to eat grass. Yum!

CHAPTER 12

Mutual Respect is Everything

*The key to every great partnership,
on and off the saddle.*

Over the two decades BeauJo and I spent together, our journey was enriched by the presence of other riders who leased him. As a vibrant and energetic horse, BeauJo thrived on activity. Balancing my roles as a professional and a mother often meant my time was stretched thin, so bringing in leasers ensured he remained engaged, fit, and content.

Side note: If you're intrigued by the equestrian world but hesitant about the full commitment of horse ownership, leasing might be your golden ticket. Think of it like dating before marriage—you get to build a relationship without diving headfirst into ownership. Many barns offer leasing options, allowing you to dip your toes (or boots) into the riding world. Take a few lessons, and who knows? You might just meet your four-legged soulmate.

Now, let me paint a picture of BeauJo for you. He was the barn's social butterfly, always poking his head out of the stall to greet anyone passing by. But he didn't stop at a simple nod—oh no. BeauJo had a whole routine. He'd bob his head up and down, flash a goofy grin, smack his lips—the full show. His charming antics earned him a fan club and, more importantly, a steady stream of treats: carrots, apples, peppermints—you name it. All well-deserved, of course.

One quirk we had to navigate was BeauJo's fondness for nibbling. It's a natural behavior in horses, rooted in their social interactions. In the wild, they engage in mutual grooming—gently biting or nibbling each other's necks and shoulders to bond and offer comfort. So when BeauJo nibbled at me, it was his way of saying, *You're part of my herd.*

But here's the catch: being orphaned as a foal, he missed out on the lessons only a horse mama can teach—like the fine line between affection and assertion. And let's be honest, human skin isn't quite as durable as horsehide.

At first, I found his nibbling endearing—a sweet sign of our growing bond. Until one sunny afternoon, after a great ride, when I was grooming him and chatting away, his playful nibble turned into a full-on bite. The pain made me jump. BeauJo startled, too. We both stared at each other in shock. The bruise that followed was so impressive my husband—ever the attorney—half-jokingly suggested we get witnesses to vouch for his innocence.

I knew BeauJo wasn't being malicious. He just needed guidance on boundaries. Over the next few months, I became more aware of his mouthy tendencies and set consistent, clear limits. It was a learning curve for both of us, but with patience and mutual respect, he adjusted. He came to understand that while his equine buddies might tolerate a nip, his human mom preferred her skin intact.

That moment became a turning point. After that, BeauJo rarely overstepped. Our bond deepened. We developed an unspoken understanding—a dance of mutual respect and trust.

With Respect Comes Trust

Over time, BeauJo and I developed a connection so deep it was like we could read each other's thoughts. On those peaceful mornings when the world was still waking up, we'd ride in the arena with nothing but the wind in the trees and the rhythm of hooves beneath us. No instructions. No pressure. Just us—tuned in and moving as one. If I so much as thought about changing direction or heading toward the poles, he was already adjusting.

And when he wasn't feeling it? I knew.

Maybe he was stiff. Maybe he was moody. Maybe he just needed a break. Instead of forcing it, we adapted. Sometimes we'd skip the saddle and play tag in the turnout. Yes, tag—with a thousand-pound horse. He'd chase me, I'd chase him. There was laughter, joy, connection. We respected each other's rhythms. And that built something strong.

A Lesson in Respect

Over the years, BeauJo had several leasers. Some were incredible. And some... taught me a lot.

One young girl stands out. She was maybe thirteen, full of energy, always rushing—like a hummingbird on espresso. Something between them wasn't clicking. So I started showing up early to watch.

She zipped through grooming, slapped on the tack, skipped the warm-up, and launched straight into her lesson like she was late to prom. Afterward, she barely patted him, tossed her gear, and was out the door.

There was no connection. No pause. No presence.

And here's the thing: horses aren't machines. They're mirrors. They reflect your energy, your intention, your presence. They don't care about your schedule or your goals. They care about how you show up.

And BeauJo? He always noticed.

At first, his resistance was subtle—a little pause at the bridle, hesitation during grooming. But soon, he was turning away in his stall, refusing to be tacked, shortening his stride, flattening his ears. The sparkle was gone. He wasn't being "bad"—he was communicating in the only language he had.

I gently tried to guide her. She didn't listen. Eventually, she moved on to another horse.

That experience stuck with me.

Because here's what I know—whether it's horses, humans, or your own damn self—you can't rush connection. You can't shortcut respect. And you sure as heck can't demand trust. It's earned. One small moment at a time, through consistency, presence, and intention.

And when you do that? That's when the rhythm clicks. That's when something beautiful grows. Not from performance—but from presence.

Because the best partnerships? They're not built in the doing. They're built in the being.

From Broken Trust to Rebuilt Strength

When I bought BeauJo, I sold my wedding ring to make it happen.

Why? Because that ring no longer held meaning. My ex-husband had shattered every vow—and in the process, shattered my self-respect. That chapter could fill a whole book of its own (ideally paired with a strong drink).

But that decision—to trade a symbol of broken promises for a new beginning—was the first brick in rebuilding my life.

BeauJo didn't just teach me to ride. He taught me to trust again.

And then came Prince Charming.

With patience, consistency, and kindness, my husband showed me what true respect looks like. He didn't rush me. He didn't overpower me. He stood beside me—steadily, quietly. What began as cautious respect became deep trust... and eventually, love.

That journey with BeauJo prepared me for the journey with my husband.

Funny how lessons from the barn show up in every corner of life.

Building Respect with Your Fellow Humans

Let's bring this home to you.

Respect isn't complicated—but it *is* intentional.

If you want to build trust with your family, your team, your clients, or even your own inner voice, ask yourself:

- Are you truly present in your conversations?
- Are you listening—or just waiting to speak?
- Are you showing up consistently—or just checking the box?
- Are you connecting—or just completing a task?

Because just like BeauJo, people feel it. They feel the rush, the distance, the disconnection. And like him, they'll respond—not always with words, but with silence, withdrawal, resistance, or burnout.

Want to build something real?

Slow down. Be present. Make eye contact. Offer your attention, not just your time. Speak with care. Listen with heart.

Don't just demand trust. Earn it.

Because **mutual respect** is the saddle that holds every great relationship together.

And when it fits just right?

You'll ride farther than you ever thought possible.

You *know* I like zippers, Mom! Up down, up down, up down!!

CHAPTER 13

Woman Plans, Horse Laughs

Because flexibility isn't just for muscles—it's for life

As a working mom, I live and die by my calendar. It's more than a schedule—it's my sanity. Like many women juggling business, babies (or teens), and everything in between, I thrive on structure. I also know it can all go sideways in a flash. Sick kid? Flat tire? Surprise school shutdown? Been there. Planned that. Adjusted anyway.

I've got two calendars—one digital, one old-school paper planner. It's a holdover from my litigation days when dual tracking was the norm. Also, as the Navy SEALs say: *Two is one. One is none.* Amen.

More than just time management, my calendar helps me protect my boundaries—especially when it comes to prioritizing my own health and wellbeing. Trust me, that lesson was earned the hard way, and I'd prefer you learn it the easy way: make time for yourself *now*. Schedule it. Block it. Keep the appointment like your life depends on it—because some-times, it does.

One of my non-negotiables? Weekly time with BeauJo, my four-legged therapist. Even with leasers riding him throughout the week, *my* time with him was sacred. We had a schedule, a routine. And when it worked? Bliss. When it didn't? Chaos.

Here's the thing—scheduling is easy. Sticking to the plan? That's where the trouble begins.

Ever planned the perfect night out—sitter locked down, dinner reservations set, movie tickets bought—only to have one of you get sick? Yeah. Me too.

So you plan. You live. You adjust.

And barn life? It's no different.

The Bridle Incident
(a.k.a. The Wardrobe Malfunction)

It was a beautiful fall morning—the kind that smells like leaves and possibilities. I rolled into the barn early, grateful for a calm day and ready for some good old-fashioned horse therapy. The air was crisp, the sun was golden, and BeauJo greeted me with that big, goofy smile he saves just for me.

Tacking up is one of my favorite rituals—half spa day, half wellness check. We take our time. He relaxes, I breathe, we connect. I brush him down, clean his hooves, double-check for cuts or scrapes. He checks me out too, as if making sure his human is still whole and sane. We've got a system.

Helmet on. Gloves secure. Time to ride.

And then it happened.

As I reached for the door, BeauJo, ever affectionate, rubbed his head along my leg. Sweet, right? Except this time, something snagged. The loop of his bridle hooked onto the belt loop of my pants. And when he lifted his head, I came with him.

Y'all—we were hooked.

Like, no-escape, locked-and-loaded, rodeo-style hooked. I was upside down on his neck, legs in the air, arms flailing, completely at his mercy.

Cue the ragdoll flops.

BeauJo panicked. I wrapped my arms around his neck like some deranged circus act. Up. Down. Up. Down. With every movement, I flailed like a sock in a washing machine. I screamed (probably), he flopped (definitely), and we both hit full "what-the-heck-is-happening" mode.

On what felt like the fourth flop, gravity finally won, and I tumbled to the ground. Miraculously, I landed like a gymnast sticking a dismount—both feet, knees bent, arms out. "I'm okay!" I declared. Because of course I did.

We both stood there, stunned. He snorted. I blinked.

And then came the breeze.

"Are you okay?" someone shouted as they ran over.

"I don't know," I said, scanning my body. Arms? Check. Legs? Check. Horse? Still standing. Check.

Then she added, deadpan, "I've got a spare pair of pants in my locker if you need them."

I looked down. Yep. My pants were shredded.

Full equestrian wardrobe malfunction.

When Life Tosses You... Saddle Up Anyway

Here's the thing about life (and horses): it rarely goes to plan. You can map it out, color-code it, put it on two calendars—and still end up upside down, pantsless, and wondering what just happened.

That's why flexibility isn't weakness—it's wisdom.

Being flexible doesn't mean being flaky. It means being present enough to adjust, grounded enough to bend without breaking, and wise enough to laugh when things go sideways.

The Yellow Cake

Prince Charming and I got married on June 21st, the longest day of the year, near the beach in Key West at the Wyndham Reach Resort. A little slice of paradise. Surrounded by our favorite people, we stood on a pier, promised to love, respect, and annoy each other forever, and watched the sun set behind us.

We planned that wedding for seven months—before Google reviews, Pinterest, or Zoom. We didn't tour the venue, sample the food, or taste the cake. Every decision was made via fax, email, or a hopeful phone call.

Thankfully, the resort assigned us a wedding planner who handled everything like a pro. I was your classic excited-but-slightly-panicked bride—held together with caffeine and color-coded lists.

The day arrived. The ceremony? Dreamy. The sunset? Perfection.

And then… the reception.

In the corner of the room, glowing like a radioactive lemon drop, stood our wedding cake.

YELLOW.

Like, *highlighter* yellow. Not just the inside—the whole thing. Bright, bold, impossible-to-miss yellow.

Now listen, I asked for *yellow cake*—on the *inside*. With ivory cream cheese frosting and raspberry filling.

Apparently, the baker took "yellow cake" as a *theme*.

My sister caught the look on my face. "What's wrong?"

I pointed. "The cake."

She blinked. "It's a cake."

I explained. She stared. And then I started laughing.

A glass of wine appeared in my hand, and just like that—I let it go.

I wasn't going to let a neon dessert hijack my happiness.

I had planned. Life laughed. And we danced anyway.

Leave Room for Life to Happen

Same with BeauJo. That day at the barn? The snagged bridle? The shredded pants? Not in the plan.

But the laughter? The lesson? The memory we'll never forget?

Absolutely in the plan.

Because no matter how tightly you hold the reins, life will remind you—you're not in control of everything. And that's okay. Michael McGriffy said it best, "Blessed are the flexible, for they shall not be bent out of shape."

So when your best-laid plans unravel, remember:

- Breathe.
- Laugh (if possible).
- Adjust the plan.
- Keep showing up.

Some of life's most meaningful moments don't happen in the plan. They live in the detours. In the flops. In the cake that glows and the bridle that bites.

That's where the magic happens.

The ride of your life *will* not go as planned...

But oh, will it be worth it.

Hey Mom – this is so fun after a bath!

CHAPTER 14

Taking the Reins

Standing Tall on Two Feet, Guided by Four.

The first time I truly stood up for myself was when I left *Idiot*—my ex-husband. That chapter of my life was dark, unhealthy, and painfully eye-opening. I felt small, dismissed, and diminished. But even in the mess, something inside me cracked open—just enough to let a little light in.

Pulling myself up by my bootstraps—or more like dragging myself by the laces—I made a bold move. Idiot told me I wasn't allowed to get a horse. So naturally... I sold the wedding ring and bought the horse.

The rebel in me roared with delight.

That decision wasn't just about a horse—it was about reclaiming my power, my voice, and my future. It was the very first step toward building a life that actually felt like mine.

Taking the Reins

During that first year with BeauJo, I was working full-time at a prestigious law firm in downtown Denver. Think: top-floor views, award-winning art, high-stakes clients flying in from all over the world, and an office energy that never slept. I supported two litigation teams led by two top-ranked partners, plus a swarm of fast-talking associates.

I also had my own office—where I tried to maintain balance and order. Spoiler alert: litigation has *zero* chill. Maintaining balance in that environment was like juggling fire while roller-skating on gravel. But oddly enough, I thrived in it. The chaos, the challenge, the pressure—I loved it. And my team knew I had their backs.

I was the go-to girl. I never said no. Need something last minute? I'm on it. Deadline moved up? I'll cancel my plans. Court brief due by midnight? You bet, I'll skip dinner. I was all in—because at the time, work was my identity. I was a recently divorced, unattached young professional just trying to prove her worth.

Then came BeauJo.

The moment he entered my life, everything shifted.

I remember that first weekend I brought him home, sitting down with my trainers and mapping out a full weekly schedule. (Shocking, I know—I love a good calendar.) BeauJo would have five lessons a week. I'd join three of them, including one every weekend. The goal? Get us both up to speed—and safe. After all, we were a green rider and a baby horse.

That Monday, I sat down with both partners to share my new schedule. Twice a week, I told them, I'd need to leave at 5 p.m. sharp.

It wasn't just a ride. It was a responsibility. A living, breathing, four-legged responsibility.

They were supportive. They smiled. They said, "Good for you."

Until one day...

A few months later, a junior associate handed me a monster-sized task at 4 p.m.—something she needed "by end of day."

I took a deep breath. This was it. The moment I had been dreading—and preparing for.

I calmly explained that I had to leave at 5, but I'd get it to her first thing in the morning. She wasn't thrilled. So off we marched to the partner's office.

He looked at me. Paused. And asked, "Is there any way you can make an exception today?"

I took another breath. "No," I said. "I have a horse—a living, breathing animal—waiting for me. I made a commitment to him, and I have to be there."

He stared at me for a long beat. The air thickened. Everyone waited to see if I'd flinch.

I didn't.

He finally turned to the associate. "Find someone else to do it," he said.

I nearly fell over. I did it. I stood up. I took the reins.

And that, my friend, was the beginning of the end. Not the end of my job—but the end of me constantly bending over backwards for everyone else. The end of treating everyone's needs like they mattered more than mine. The end of pretending I didn't have a life beyond the office.

The truth? I didn't know how to prioritize me... until BeauJo taught me.

The First of Many "No's"

That wasn't the end. It was just the beginning.

And not everyone clapped when I started choosing my priorities over their expectations. The asks kept coming. The pressure didn't stop. But I stood tall anyway. As Prentis Hemphill said, "Boundaries are the distance at which I can love you and me simultaneously."

Because once you know what matters most, it's up to you to protect it.

Boundaries are like reins—they give you direction, focus, and control. But here's the kicker: the movement? That comes from your legs. That's where the power is. Just like in riding.

Knowing what you stand for is one thing. Backing it up with action? That's where the real growth happens.

Over time, saying no became easier. I started asking myself: Is this a priority—or an obligation? Am I doing this from alignment—or from guilt?

I stopped showing up for everyone else at the expense of myself. What began as protecting time with BeauJo turned into something deeper: honoring my voice, my energy, my dreams.

I started keeping the promises I made—to him, to others, and most importantly… to myself.

Because taking the reins isn't about controlling your life—it's about owning it.

It's about committing to what matters. Showing up for others without abandoning yourself.

You Don't Need Permission

I didn't know how to prioritize myself until a horse showed me how. And later, becoming a mother solidified that strength.

But let me tell you this: you don't need a horse or a child to be your reason.

You are reason enough.

If you've been waiting for permission, consider this it.

Start where you are.

Know what matters.

Take the reins.

Hold them with clarity.

And when it's time—kick into action.

You don't need to justify your priorities to anyone.

You just need to live them.

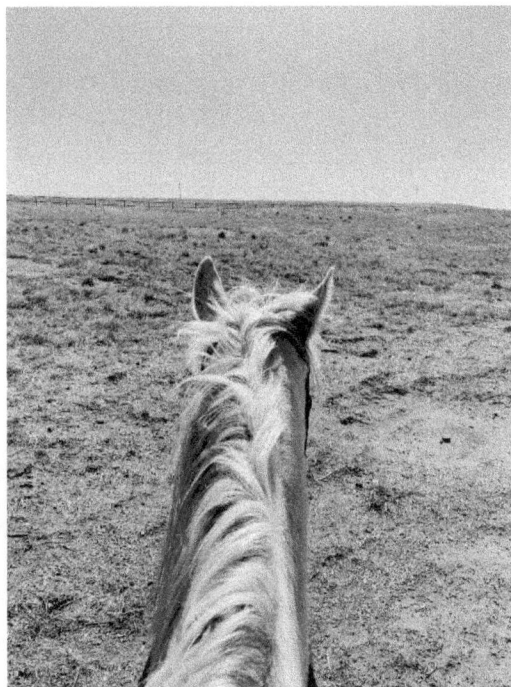

The best view ever!

CHAPTER 15

Horse Heal Thy Heart

Discovering the best therapy comes with hooves.

B eauJo came into my life at a time when I was desperate to feel seen, steady, and unconditionally loved. After a gut-wrenching divorce that shook me to my core—mentally, physically, and spiritually—I was drowning in shame and self-doubt. It felt like I'd been bucked off the ride of life and landed face-first in a pile of emotional manure.

Therapy helped. Truly. It gave me the tools to leave a toxic marriage and begin putting myself first. I started to see glimpses of my strength again. But even after months of doing "the work," there was still a void—a tender space inside me that no amount of talking could quite touch.

Then came BeauJo.

I had no idea at the time how much that four-legged goofball would change everything. What started as a dream turned into a lifeline. It wasn't just about grooming or riding or training—it was about healing. Quietly. Honestly. From the inside out. With BeauJo, I didn't have to explain, defend, or smile through the pain. I didn't have to pretend. I could just *be*—messy, uncertain, raw, and real.

The barn became my safe space. My breath. My church. And BeauJo? He was the minister of grace I didn't know I needed.

Some days, I would cry into his mane, letting the tears fall with no need for translation. Some days, we'd walk in silence, just the two of us, side by side. Other days, I'd talk to him like he was my therapist—and he'd listen better than most humans ever could.

If I needed to fall apart, the barn was a safe place. If I needed to quiet the chaos in my head, it was a safe place. If I just wanted to be with someone who expected absolutely nothing from me, it was the safest place of all.

Over time, showing up at the barn meant showing up for *me*.

It wasn't about progress. It was about presence. It wasn't about being fixed. It was about being *felt*.

He became my sanctuary. My mirror. My heart-healer.

BeauJo helped me rebuild not just my confidence—but my spirit. He never judged the woman who showed up. He just stood there, steady and still, and waited for me to meet myself again. With each ride, each quiet grooming session, each belly-deep breath I took in his presence, I came home to myself.

He taught me the language of energy. The magic of stillness. The deep power of connection without words.

And here's what I know now: healing isn't always loud. Sometimes it comes in silence. In routine. In rhythm. In the soft brush of a muzzle or the quiet nod of a horse who *just knows*.

BeauJo didn't just help me find my way back—he helped shape the woman, the mother, and the leader I've become.

And the most beautiful part? I wasn't the only one.

Over the years, others who had the chance to ride or lease BeauJo found their own healing in his presence. That's the magic of horses—they don't fix you, but somehow, they help you remember how to fix yourself.

One such individual was a middle school student who leased BeauJo during a pivotal time in her life. She affectionately called him "Beau," and their time together was nothing short of transformative.

As a mom, you just know when your children—even the four-legged ones—are with the right people. Erin was the right person for BeauJo, and he was the right horse for her.

In her own words, Erin shares their story:

> I had the absolute honor of riding and loving BeauJo for a good chunk of my life—eight unforgettable years. He wasn't just a horse; he was my safe space, my escape, my best friend. And the best part? We didn't even need words.
>
> When I first met Beau, I was in a really tough spot. My dad had passed away two years prior, and things at home were rough—my mom and I were constantly at odds. But Beau was my anchor. The moment I walked into the barn, everything heavy seemed to lift. He always had that signature goofy smile, shoving his head into my space just to make sure I saw it. And somehow, I always smiled back.
>
> Beau never hurt a soul. Sure, I fell off him a few times— what rider hasn't? But I'll never forget one fall in particular: he could have stepped on me, but he dodged me with such intention. That's who he was. Loyal. Kind. A gentle soul in a giant body.
>
> One day stands out more than the rest. I was having an awful day—school was brutal, I was fighting with my mom, and I didn't even want to ride. But as soon as I stepped into

his turnout, he came right over to me. No stops for grass. No hesitation. He just *knew*. That entire lesson, he took care of me. He always did—whether we were synced up or bickering like siblings, he showed up for me.

There are so many memories I hold close to my heart, because Beau wasn't just a part of my life—he helped shape who I am. Even on the days I didn't ride, just being near him healed something in me. Watching him run free (or chasing him to get him to run—classic) made everything feel better.

He had such a beautiful soul. And while he may have had a few awkward features here and there, to me, he was pure beauty—inside and out.

BeauJo made me a better rider, yes. But more than that, he made me a better person. He taught me patience. How to love. How to loosen up and laugh. And how to not take life too seriously.

I know I'll never meet another horse like him. I was so incredibly blessed to have had that time. I'll forever miss him—and the version of myself I was when I was with him.

Thank you for sharing him with me.

– Erin Feeley

The Silent Strength of the Herd

They say healing isn't linear—and neither is the path to it. For many of us, especially those who have served or supported others through trauma, traditional therapy can feel like trying to speak a language we never learned. But horses? They speak in silence, in presence, in truth. They don't need words to understand us. They feel us.

Michelle's Story: Trust, Leadership, and Authentic Connection

As Michelle L. Kaye, MA, LPC, Founder and Executive Director of Operation Equine—a nonprofit dedicated to empowering military service members, veterans, first responders, and their families through equine-assisted therapy—shares:

"The horse will teach you if you will listen." — Roy Hunt

For the past 12 years, I've had the honor of working exclusively with active military service members, veterans, first responders, and their families. As a civilian, earning the trust of this community has been a journey—one that mirrors the process of building trust with horses. Every single interaction is an opportunity to earn that trust again.

People often ask me, "Why horses?" Especially when I explain who I serve. The answer lies in the feedback they give—immediate, visceral, and undeniable. You don't just *see* it; you *feel* it. Something shifts in your bones, and you are never the same afterward.

I remember one veteran—let's call him Joe—who showed up to a session with flat eyes and no expression. The activity was simple: choose a horse, walk him on a lead rope, and then try again without the rope. Joe, a leader in the Army, was used to following and giving orders. When he led Preacher, a well-trained horse, with the rope, Preacher followed—because he was asked to. But the moment the rope came off, Preacher followed only a few steps before wandering off. Again and again.

Joe stood there, growing more frustrated, as the other participants' horses willingly followed their humans without ropes—because they *wanted* to, not because they *had* to.

His face got tight. He stopped breathing. I walked over and asked him, "Joe, what do you *really* want in your life?"

Without hesitation, he said, "I want this horse to follow me."

I smiled and asked again, "Not just here... what do you want for your *life*?"

He paused, then said, "My career. I want to feel clear and successful again."

I asked him to embody it—really feel what it would be like to achieve that success. To imagine the paycheck, the clothes, the clients, the confidence. His shoulders pulled back. His walk became purposeful. His breath deepened.

And that's when Preacher started to follow him.

Step for step. No rope. Just energy. Just presence.

Joe looked back.

"Don't look back," I told him. "He's there. Trust what you're feeling."

Joe picked up the pace. So did Preacher. Joe smiled wider. Preacher walked faster.

They completed three laps, in perfect sync, without a single tool or prompt—just trust and clarity. When they stopped, they did so together.

Joe's eyes were bright. He looked at me and said, "I *felt* it."

And on his way out that day, he added, "Nothing else has worked. THIS worked."

Trust. Leadership. Authentic connection.

These are not just keys to working with horses—they're essential to healing, growth, and every healthy relationship, including the one we have with ourselves.

Our brains may be bigger, but horses' hearts are larger—literally and figuratively. They can feel our heartbeat from up to four feet away. And when we slow down enough to meet them in presence, their heartbeat can entrain with ours. It can calm us. Ground us. Heal us.

Horses are sentient beings with thoughts, feelings, and opinions of their own. As herd animals, their survival depends on connection. They require communication, clarity, and presence. If your mind is scattered, they'll know—and they'll walk away. But when they choose to walk *with* you, because they feel something real?

That's connection. That's healing. That's transformation.

And that moment stays with you—forever.

The Silent Strength of the Horses

What started as one woman's journey through heartbreak and healing became something so much greater. BeauJo wasn't just my therapy—he was a gift I got to share. His steady presence left footprints on the hearts of every person who walked beside him, reminding us all that healing doesn't always come from words or wisdom—it often comes from simply being seen and accepted, just as you are.

If you're walking through your own valley right now—grief, trauma, heartbreak, uncertainty—know this: you don't have to do it alone. Maybe your healing doesn't look like a saddle and reins. Maybe it looks like a quiet walk, a warm hug, a deep breath, or an open heart. Whatever it looks like, let it be yours.

The path to wholeness isn't about fixing what's broken. It's about remembering who you've always been—and letting love, in all its forms, lead you back to yourself.

Be still. Be open. Be brave.

And when in doubt?

Find your barn. Find your BeauJo. Or whatever brings you peace. Because healing doesn't happen in one big breakthrough.

It happens in the quiet.

In the presence.

In the love that never asks for anything in return—just that you keep showing up.

Day by day.

Step by step.

Heart to hoof.

You had me at hello.

CHAPTER 16

Fall Seven Times, Rise Eight

Embrace the grit to get back on.

I've been bullied, accused of stealing, pushed around, fired, cheated on, lied to—the list goes on. With each blow, a little piece of me chipped away, leaving me feeling smaller and more fragmented.

Then came BeauJo.

From our very first lesson, my trainer set the expectation: anticipate falling off, getting kicked, bitten, stepped on—or worse.

"Know this," she would say. "It will happen. And when it does? It doesn't matter. You get back on. You keep going. You adjust. You figure it out."

Get Back in the Saddle.

From that moment forward, I made a pact with myself: never end a ride on a defeat. If I fell off, I got back on. If BeauJo refused a jump, we circled back and did it again. If he tried to buck me off, we paused, recalibrated, and moved forward.

I refused to let us end on a bad note.

About ten years into our partnership, BeauJo and I had developed a comfortable rhythm. I was still refining my seat and skills (well, that never really ends), and one crisp Sunday morning, we set out on a trail ride with two friends. The air was tinged with autumn, the sun was shining, and both humans and horses were in high spirits—a perfect day.

We headed toward a trail that featured three downed trees, spaced just right for jumping. It was my favorite path: secluded, with low obstacles that made for easy, joyful jumps. We warmed up our horses along the way, transitioning from a walk to a trot. By the time we reached the trees, both riders and horses were in sync. We each cleared the obstacles smoothly, smiles all around, and continued toward a familiar stream.

After crossing the water, the path led to a hill we had navigated many times before. But that morning, it was still slick from the night's rain. Horses are generally surefooted, even in mud—but not always.

My two friends ascended the hill without issue. I followed, but as if in slow motion, BeauJo lost his footing. His hooves slipped. His weight shifted. He began to roll.

Realizing what was happening, I quickly pulled my feet from the stirrups and rolled to the right to avoid being crushed.

It all happened so fast—yet felt like slow motion.

I rolled one way; BeauJo rolled the other. We both sprang up, looked at each other like, "You okay?"

My friends returned to check on us, and we all burst into laughter. I was half-covered in mud; BeauJo, of course, was spotless.

After confirming we were both unhurt, I found a rock to mount from (short-girl problems) and got back in the saddle. We finished the ride a little shaken, a little sore—but in one piece and ready for a treat.

I Got Back in the Saddle.

And that, my friend, is life.

Every time I lost a job—I got back in the saddle.

Every time my company shut its doors and I had to start over—I got back in the saddle.

Every time I heard we weren't pregnant—I got back in the saddle.

Every time I lost a customer—I got back in the saddle.

Every time my Itty-Bitty Shitty Committee piped up—I got back in the saddle.

This isn't just about courage or determination—it's about *grit*. It's about refusing to give in, refusing to stay down, and knowing that every fall carries a lesson.

And just like my trainer told me back then, I'll tell you now:

You will get knocked off. It's not *if*—it's *when*. And when it happens, you don't freeze. You don't flail. You *get back on*.

Show Up, Even When It's Messy

Grit isn't about looking polished—it's about showing up anyway. It's brushing yourself off when your heart's heavy and your coffee's cold. It's choosing progress over perfection. One shaky step forward still counts as forward.

So What If You Don't Feel Like It? Do It Anyway

Let's be honest—waiting to "feel like it" is a trap. Motivation is flaky. But discipline? That's your ride-or-die.

The truth is, you don't need to feel it to do it. You just need to do it.

- You don't need to feel ready—you need to *be* ready.
- You don't need motivation—you need *commitment*.
- You don't need to want to—you just need to *start*.

Because action creates momentum. One step leads to another. And grit? Grit shows up when you do.

Flip the Script on Failure

You're going to fall. You're going to mess up. But that's not the end—it's the lesson.

Instead of asking, "Why did this happen to me?"

Ask: "What did this teach me?"

Every stumble is a stepping stone. Every misstep is a message.

Fall seven times. Rise eight.

As Gary Ryan Blair said: *"You didn't come this far to only come this far. Dig deep. Finish strong. Make yourself proud."*

So saddle up. Tighten the girth. Wipe off the dirt. And keep going.

Because the strength you seek—your grit—is already within you, just waiting to be unleashed.

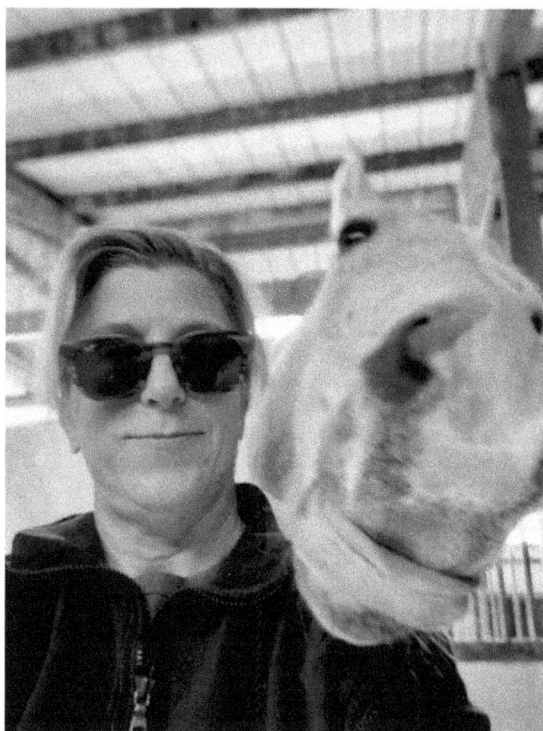

Peppermint me, please!

CHAPTER 17

Parting is Such Sweet Sorrow

For the one who changed everything.

When you find yourself at the end of something beautiful, it's natural to reflect on its beginning. From the very first day with BeauJo, I knew that our journey together would one day lead to a painful goodbye. Our cherished pets, those joyful and loving companions, grace our lives for only a fraction of our own lifetimes, making each farewell an inevitable heartache.

In BeauJo's final days, my heart swirled with memories—of our first meeting, the bond we forged, and the countless moments that defined our journey. He was more than a horse; he was my sanctuary, my teacher, and my steadfast companion. Now, I faced the heart-wrenching task of saying goodbye.

Over two decades, we matured together. We laughed, learned, healed, and faced hardships. He gained weight; I gained wisdom. I trained his body; he nurtured my soul.

BeauJo wasn't just a horse; he was my partner, my mirror, my best friend.

The last six months of his life were slow, sacred, and filled with love. We no longer rode; instead, we wandered, walked, and played. He'd roll in the sunshine like a playful pup and beg for peppermints with his signature charm. I watched the tumors grow and the spark in his eyes begin to fade. Deep down, I knew I had to prioritize his peace over my impending pain.

I hoped for a miracle, but it didn't come.

On a beautiful April day in 2024, we shared our final walk, our last peppermint, and a quiet moment of connection. I whispered everything I needed to say, though I knew he already understood.

I've bid farewell to beloved animals before—cherished dogs and dear pets—but this was different. BeauJo had been by my side for 22 years, longer than I've been a mother. He was family. He raised me as much as I raised him, shaping me into the woman, mother, business owner, and leader I am today.

Explaining the depth of such a bond to someone who hasn't experienced it is challenging. Animals offer us immeasurable gifts, often beyond our comprehension. And BeauJo? He gave me everything.

This book—and every lesson within—is dedicated to him. My handsome boy. My big man. My once-in-a-lifetime "boyfriend."

People often ask if I'll get another horse. Every time, my answer remains: No. He was my one.

Yet, if BeauJo taught me anything, it's that life has a way of surprising us with unexpected joy. So... I never say never.

BeauJo—until we meet again on the other side of this life, thank you. For your love, patience, sass, and soul. For guiding me, grounding me, and growing with me. You are forever in my heart, a part of every choice I make, every lesson I teach, every time I take the reins.

May the fields be green, the skies vast, and the trails soft beneath your hooves.

Giddy up, my love. Run free.

Navigating Grief

Losing a cherished animal is a profound experience, and the journey through grief is deeply personal. Here are some insights and suggestions to help others cope with such a loss:

- Honor Your Feelings: Allow yourself to fully experience the range of emotions that come with loss. Suppressing grief can prolong the healing process.

- Create a Tribute: Consider writing a letter to your pet, compiling a photo album, planting a tree, or even authoring a book in their memory. These acts can provide a tangible way to celebrate their life.

- Seek Support: Connect with friends, family, or support groups who understand the depth of your loss. Sharing stories and feelings can be therapeutic.

- Be Patient with Yourself: Grieving doesn't follow a set timeline. Allow yourself the grace to heal at your own pace.

Remember, there's no "right" way to grieve.

If you are grieving right now, I see you.

It's a deeply personal journey, and it's okay to seek help and create rituals that resonate with you. BeauJo will live on in this book. Your pet's memory will live on in your heart, and honoring that bond in your unique way can be a comforting step toward healing.

Don't Cry for the Horses *by Brenda Riley-Seymore*

Don't cry for the horses that life has set free.
A million white horses forever to be.
Don't cry for the horses now in God's hand.
As they dance and they prance in a heavenly band.

They were ours as a gift, but never to keep.
As they close their eyes forever to sleep.
Their spirits unbound. On silver wings they fly.
A million white horses against the blue sky.

Look up into heaven, you'll see them above.
The horses we lost, the horses we loved.
Manes and tails flowing, they gallop through time.
They were never yours - they were never mine.

Don't cry for the horses. They'll be back someday.
When our time is gone, they will show us the way.
Do you hear that soft nicker? Close to your ear?
Don't cry for the horses. Love the ones that are here.

CHAPTER 18

Conclusion

Embracing the ride of life, today and always.

As we draw the reins on this journey together, it's time to reflect on the path we've traveled. From those tentative first steps into the stable to the exhilarating gallops across open fields, each chapter has highlighted the transformative power of horses and the profound lessons they impart.

Harnessing Strength

Horses, with their majestic presence, teach us about inner fortitude. They show us that true strength isn't about dominance but about understanding and mutual respect. As Walter Zettl wisely said, "The goal of all dressage riding should be to bring the horse and rider together in harmony...a oneness of balance, purpose, and athletic expression."

Overcoming Obstacles

Life, much like riding, presents its share of hurdles. Whether it's a fallen log on a trail or unforeseen challenges in our personal journey, the key is to approach them with grace and determination. Remember, "The hardest thing about riding... is the ground!" But each fall teaches us resilience and the importance of getting back in the saddle.

Reins of Responsibility

Taking the reins symbolizes more than guiding a horse; it's about taking charge of our destiny. It's a reminder that while we can't control every twist and turn, we can choose our response. As the saying goes, "A horse doesn't care how much you know until he knows how much you care."

Savoring the Journey

In our pursuit of goals, it's easy to focus solely on the destination. Yet, horses teach us the joy of the ride—the beauty of the present moment. They remind us to breathe, to feel, and to connect deeply with the world around us. After all, "In riding a horse, we borrow freedom."

Embracing the 'Of HORSE I Can' Spirit

As you close this book, carry forward the spirit "Of HORSE I Can." Let it be a mantra that propels you to:

- Harness your inner strength.
- Overcome challenges with grace.

- **R**espect yourself and others.
- **S**eize each day with enthusiasm.
- **E**mbrace the journey wholeheartedly.

A Call to Action

Now, dear reader, it's your turn. Reflect on the lessons shared, saddle up with determination, and embark on your unique journey. Whether you're navigating life's trails or forging new paths, remember that with the right mindset and a dash of horse-inspired wisdom, there's no obstacle too great.

So, tighten your girth, adjust your stirrups, and ride forward with confidence. The horizon awaits, and the adventure is yours to command.

Giddy up!

About the Author

CEO | Speaker | Author |
Leadership & Communication Coach

Cathy Reilly is the CEO of Sharing the Shine, a company founded on the belief that when individuals embrace their authentic selves, they shine. As a globally recognized inspirational speaker, transformative trainer, and podcast host, Cathy has empowered organizations such as Anthem, Costco, and T-Mobile. Her insights have been featured on esteemed platforms including the LA Tribune and eWomen Network.

Specializing in emotional intelligence, personal leadership, effective communication, and mindset mastery, Cathy draws upon her extensive background in psychology, neurolinguistics, business, and law to inspire meaningful change. With over three decades of experience, she equips leaders to unlock their potential, navigate change with confidence, and foster sustainable growth. Cathy firmly believes that true success begins from within, empowering individuals and teams to harness their inner strength and take bold, intentional steps toward excellence every day.

She is the Amazon best-selling author of *Unleash Your Inner Voice: An Introvert's Guide to Overcoming the Itty-Bitty Shitty Committee* and the host of the *Breaking Bad Communication* podcast. Cathy serves on the board for Colorado Business Women, as a Premier Success Coach for eWomen Network, and Alpha Speaker Pro Leader for Achieve Business Systems.

In her spare time, Cathy enjoys paddleboarding, golfing, and running with her puppy through the scenic hills of Colorado.

"Of HORSE I Can" is more than a title or phrase—it's a declaration of resilience, transformation, and the profound healing that occurs when we allow ourselves to be seen, felt, and guided by the wisdom of horses.

In my journey, horses have been my sanctuary, my mirror, and my heart-healer.

Stirrup Some Inspiration

"To ride on a horse is to fly without wings." — Author Unknown

"A great horse will change your life. The truly special ones define it..." — Author Unknown

"Courage is being scared to death... and saddling up anyway." — *John Wayne*

"The essential joy of being with horses is that it brings us in contact with the rare elements of grace, beauty, spirit, and freedom." — *Sharon Ralls Lemon*

"To be yourself in a world that is constantly trying to make you something else is the greatest accomplishment." — *Ralph Waldo Emerson*

"People often say that motivation doesn't last. Well, neither does bathing—that's why we recommend it daily." — *Zig Ziglar*

"Life is getting up one more time than you've been knocked down." — *John Wayne*

"Grit is having the courage to push through, no matter what the obstacles are, because it's worth it." — *Chris Morri*

"No hour of life is wasted that is spent in the saddle." — Winston Churchill

"The wind of heaven is that which blows between a horse's ears." — *Arabian Proverb*

"There's something about the outside of a horse that is good for the inside of a man." —Winston Churchill

"People with grit don't believe that failure is a permanent condition." — *Angela Duckworth*

"All battles are fought by scared men who'd rather be some place else." — *John Wayne*

"When you come against trouble, it's never half as bad if you face up to it." — *John Wayne*

"It is much easier to ride a horse in the direction it is going." — Abraham Lincoln

"The horse is a mirror to your soul." — *Buck Brannaman*

"Slap some bacon on a biscuit and let's go! We're burnin' daylight!" — *John Wayne*

See you on the trails… Giddy up!

Why Book Cathy Reilly for Your Next Event?

Cathy Reilly isn't just a speaker—she's a catalyst for transformation. With over three decades of experience, Cathy has empowered leaders and teams at organizations like Anthem, Costco, and T-Mobile to unlock their potential, navigate change with confidence, and cultivate a culture of success through effective communication. Her dynamic approach blends emotional intelligence, personal leadership, and mindset mastery, leaving audiences not only inspired but equipped with actionable strategies to foster sustainable growth.

Cathy's authenticity, humor, and relatable storytelling create an engaging atmosphere where attendees feel seen, heard, and motivated to take bold, intentional steps toward excellence. Whether she's addressing the challenges of the "Itty-Bitty Shitty Committee" or guiding leaders to harness their inner strength, Cathy delivers messages that resonate long after the event concludes.

If you're seeking a speaker who can ignite passion, promote growth, and help build a communication-driven culture of excellence—Cathy Reilly is the voice your audience needs to hear.

www.SharingtheShine.com
creilly@sharingtheshine.com